Paul Revere and the Minutemen

A Narrative Poem by Carole Charles

pictures by Bob Seible

THE CHILD'S WORLD ELGIN, ILLINOIS 60120

For months, Bostonians had been smuggling weapons and ammunition and supplies out of Boston. General Gage, the British governor, knew this was so. He also knew the arms were stored at Concord. He devised a secret plan to capture these supplies.

His secret was soon known to the Minutemen, who waited to warn everyone if Gage's troops moved.

April 18, 1775, is the night of Paul Revere's ride. Another courier, William Dawes, also rode to warn the Minutemen. Long before the British soldiers reached Concord, the weapons and ammunition were hidden in the woods, and Minutemen were ready to fight.

The battles at Lexington and Concord, which took place on April 19, are the actual beginning of the Revolutionary War.

Library of Congress Cataloging in Publication Data

Charles, Carole, 1943-
 Paul Revere and the Minutemen.

 (Stories of the Revolution)
 SUMMARY: Narrates the reasons for Paul Revere's ride and the subsequent confrontations between the British and the Minutemen which in effect began the Revolutionary War.
 1. Revere, Paul, 1735-1818—Juvenile poetry.
2. United States—History—Revolution, 1775-1783—Juvenile poetry. [1. Revere, Paul, 1735-1818—Poetry.
2. United States—History—Revolution, 1775-1783—Poetry] I. Seible, Bob. II. Title.
PZ8.3.C383Pau   811'.5'4   75-33204
ISBN 0-913778-19-2

Distributed by Childrens Press, 1224 West Van Buren Street, Chicago, Illinois 60607

Paul Revere
and the
Minutemen

Listen, children, and I'll tell you a story
About Paul Revere and his ride to
    glory...
How he rode to Lexington one dark
    night
To call the Minutemen out to fight.

Paul lived two hundred years ago,
When life was hard and news was slow—
No cars, no planes, no phones, of course.
Paul took the news around by horse.

Paul was a rebel, a patriot was he.
He wanted the country to be free.
The rebels were tired of British rule,
Of soldiers telling them what to do.

The rebels talked and thought, and then
They started a group of Minutemen

Who had one minute to dress and arm
If British soldiers came for harm.
In just one minute they'd be out the
    door,
Ready to fight, ready for war.

The British laughed. "What soldiers are these?
Their farmers' clothes have holes in the knees!
How could they fight an army like ours?
They'd better stick to growing flowers!"

But these Minutemen were soldiers all;
They promised they would be on call.
Each kept his gun right by his side,
So even at night he was ready to ride.

On a dark, dark night, real trouble began
When the rebels learned of the British plan.
"They're after the ammunition we stored;
The British are ready to march to Concord!"

Paul quietly rowed across the bay.
He had arranged a signal that day.

"If the British cross by land tonight,
In that church tower you'll see one light.

"But if they cross the bay instead,
Then two lights will be there," he'd said.
"A horse must be ready, so I can ride
As soon as I get to the other side.
The Minutemen will have to know!"
Paul's friend watched. He saw two lights aglow!

The horse was waiting on the other side;
All was ready for Paul Revere's ride.
He called at every farmhouse door,
"The British are coming!" then rode some more.

Next morning the British came into sight
And a group of Minutemen lined up to fight.
But the British outnumbered them, ten to one.
The skirmish was over, though just begun.

The British marched to Concord Square,
Then sent men searching everywhere.
The battle began on the Concord Bridge,
With rebels advancing from the ridge.
The Minutemen hid behind rocks and big trees;
They crawled on their stomachs, shot from their knees.

The British never had fought in this way.
No time to take aim! They ran every way!

Thus the Revolutionary War did start
With each rebel fighting with all his heart,
Risking his life so he could be free,
Passing that freedom to you and to me.